Social Media Marketing

Build Your Online Business, Brand and Influence In 2019 By Marketing And Advertising on Instagram, Facebook, YouTube, Twitter And Pinterest To Scale Your Audience And Network

Max Plitt

consent and can in no way be considered an endorsement from the trademark holder.

Table of Contents

Introduction

The Importance of Social Media

If you are a small business owner, then one of your most important partners will be social media. Social media has become a crucial business tool for all businesses. According to statistics, over 90% of all marketers agree that social media has helped increase their online exposure. No matter what you are selling and who your customers are, the use of social media as a marketing tool will increase your profits and enhance your brand.

Social media platforms enable you to connect with your buyers, enhances your brand awareness, and boosts sales and leads. There are more than 3 billion people around the world using social media each month and targeting this large market regularly is definitely not just a trend.

While it is essential, not everyone understands everything about social media marketing. This is alright as you do not need to know and understand complex buzzwords and phrases used in the industry. It is advisable to get started with social media as soon as you can. Here are some reasons why social media is important.

1. Create awareness: As an online business owner, you need to get the word out there about your business. If people are unaware of your business, how will they then become customers? Fortunately, social media enhances your brand name and boosts your visibility among potential customers. This allows you to reach a wide audience through your campaign efforts.

2. Define your social media strategy: You need to take a moment and develop a sound social media strategy. The strategy should define exactly what you hope to achieve. For instance, what is your aim? Do you want to attract new customers to your website? Do you wish to increase your profits? Or perhaps brand exposure? When your strategy is specific, you will be able to determine the best social media channels for your business.

There are lots of other positive attributes of social media. For instance, you can use it to show your brand's authenticity, to communicate authority, to provide support to your customers, encourage engagement, and also allow your business to grow at an affordable rate.

Any Business Can Use Social Media

It is a fact that any business can make use of social media. It is not a preserve of large corporations or financially stable businesses. There are plenty of social media platforms that you can choose. All you need to do is to identify which one of these platforms is most suitable for your needs. Opening an account or brand page on social media is free and you can add as much information and as many photos as you want.

Once your business is established, you should get it onto various social media. These include Facebook, Twitter, Instagram, Pinterest, and YouTube among others. Remember that it is free to do so but the benefits can be huge for your business.

Organic Versus Paid Results

Anytime users enter search terms into a search engine such as Google, they are likely to receive two different types of results. These are organic results and paid results. Organic results are also known as natural results. Organic outcomes of search engines are as a result of SEO techniques used so anyone who optimizes their website appropriately gets to rank high on search results.

We can safely declare that organic search results are websites and web page listings that closely match the search terms entered by a web user. The results are often ranked so that the most relevant outcomes are listed at the top.

Paid results are essentially advertisements that people have to pay so that their web pages are displayed when certain terms or phrases are entered into a search engine. Therefore, paid listings will appear when a person runs a search query containing certain keywords.

It is easy to tell the difference between organic and paid outcomes. First of all, search engines separate them and list the paid ones at the top. Sometimes paid results are displayed on the right-hand side of the screen. Other times, they will be displayed on a shaded background. Some search engines even indicate paid outcomes so that users are aware.

Organic outcomes are more important

Ideally, you will want to rely more on organic outcomes because these are as a result of hard work on the part of a business owner. They display the best results based on analysis by sophisticated search software. The search engines use powerful algorithms to identify websites with the most relevant content. You can always count on the results to find exactly what you are searching for.

Sometimes web users may not be able to tell the difference between paid and organic search outcomes. As such, they may not be able to make informed decisions. As an online business owner, you need to learn how to be able to obtain results from both sources. This means learning all about search engine optimization for organic outcomes and search engine marketing for paid outcomes.

You Should Post Regularly on Social Media

As a business owner, you need to be aware of the power of social media and its ability to drive traffic to your website, as well as increase conversion rates. If you want to successfully tap into this power and impact of social media, then you need to invest effort, time, and money.

One of the best ways is to engage your readers. You can post content on social media regularly and invite them to share their thoughts and opinions. It will be difficult in the initial stages because you will first have to create a following. Therefore, ensure that you invest lots of time, energy, and resources into building one.

Once you have a reasonable following, you should maintain regular posting because this supports your business in numerous ways. For instance, you will increase the visibility of your business as well as brand awareness. You will need to create content then share it with others. Content here means any text message, image, or video. Remember to respond to comments and queries from your followers and from all other web visitors.

Other benefits you will receive because of regular posting include better lead conversion rates, better rankings on search engines results, and brand loyalty. You will also be able to maintain customer interest in your brand and products, customer satisfaction, and handle any issues of public relations. This means easily resolving customer complaints and providing them with advice and information on your different products or services.

Chapter 1: Social Media Marketing for Businesses

Social media marketing is an important pathway for all kinds of businesses to interact with customers and prospects. As it is, your customers are probably already interacting with other brands via popular social media sites. Therefore, you should also be speaking to them, posting content, and interacting on these social networking sites otherwise you will lose out.

Some of the more popular social websites include Instagram, Pinterest, Twitter, YouTube, Facebook, and Google. If you have an online business, make sure that you get it onto one or more of these platforms. Social media can bring you remarkable success and supply you with devoted brand advocates. You will also be able to handle additional matters via social media including sales, customer services, and so on.

What is Social Media Marketing?

Social media marketing is a kind of internet marketing technique. It involves the creation of content and sharing it on social media platforms with friends, followers, and the general public. There are hundreds of millions of social media users around the world. Attracting them to your business via social media is essentially what social media marketing is all about.

Some common activities associated with social media marketing include posting relevant videos, uploading written posts, and updating images. You post all these in order to entice your viewers, readers, and followers. When you engage them, answer their questions, or respond to their comments, you gain credibility and they begin to trust in you. Driving audience engagement and placing paid advertisements are also crucial aspects of social media marketing.

Marketing strategies for small businesses

A lot of small business owners are careful about where they spend their money. They choose carefully the marketing strategies that they invest in mostly because they have a limited budget and wish to get as much out of their investments as possible.

It is advisable as a small business owner to spend wisely in order to get the best returns. One of the most effective ways of doing this is marketing through social media platforms. This kind of approach is versatile with cost-effective strategies that actually work. It is no wonder that over 97% of all marketers use social media as most of their customers and potential customers are on one or more of these platforms.

Your customers are on social media

One of the reasons why you should market your small business is that your customers are on social media and spending considerable amounts of time each day. According to reliable statistics, over 70% of US residents are on one social media platform or other. The number of social media users around the world is expected to increase to about 2.5 billion this year. Since so many consumers are using social media, it only makes sense to reach out to them. Social media provides small businesses with an opportunity to reach out to a wide audience.

Consumers are more responsive on social media

It has been established that consumers are more receptive of marketing messages on social media than most other platforms. The reason is that social networking websites provide a fun and exciting way to interact, network, and keep in touch with friends and family. While users do not necessarily get online to receive marketing messages from businesses, they are very receptive especially when approached in an engaging and interactive manner. Most consumers on social media are happy to interact with their favorite brands.

Brand recognition on social media

One of the main benefits of social media is that it helps small business owners improve the visibility of their brands and products. When visibility is enhanced, your brand gets recognition and acceptance by your viewers and followers. You need to create business social media profiles across different platforms because these will open new doors and present new and exciting opportunities. You get to share content and also present your brand's personality and voice.

You need to make sure that you post compelling content including articles, videos, and photos that add value to your viewers. This way, you will be ensuring that your brand is accessible and customers are familiar with it. As an example, think about an online user who comes across your posts. They may not be aware of you or your business and brand, but the content may be compelling enough. As a result, this person may like your product and possibly share it with his network of about 200 to 500 friends and followers.

Build Your Own Personal Brand

When you share content online, you get an amazing opportunity to create an online persona. This persona generally reflects your professional skills as well as personal values. Many business owners use social media only as a platform to put out their brands and products. Many others gain useful connections, crucial leads, and eventually faithful followers and customers.

Here are some steps that you can follow in order to successfully build your brand and promote on social media. By doing so, you will increase your reach and following, catch the eye of consumers, and basically gain a huge following within a short time.

1. Carefully select then update your preferred social networks

There are a number of social media accounts out there. You need to choose two or three of the most important based on certain criteria like preference and so on. Once you choose your preferred social media accounts, you should then fully update them including your business name, address, brands, and then add content of all kind. If you have any old accounts that you are no longer using, then close them down or delete them.

It is crucial that you update your current accounts with relevant content and accurate information. This way, you will be able to build traffic to your social network pages that you wish to share. It also provides you with an opportunity to remove any unnecessary or unsuitable content that does not reflect well about you.

2. Share content regularly

It is advisable to ensure that you share relevant and engaging content with your followers on a regular basis. However, you have to differentiate between sharing engaging and relevant content with spammy posts and over-posting. When you post too many times, your followers will consider this to be annoying and spammy. You want to keep your followers engaged and to keep communication lines open. However, over-sharing makes you seem tacky and desperate. The ideal situation is posting between 3 and 4 times per week then responding to comments, queries, and questions about your posts.

As experts have pointed out, a single post on social media will not help you to achieve much. This is why it is advisable to post content on different social websites a couple of times per week. For instance, you can post 3 to 4 times on Facebook, Instagram, and Twitter then follow the posts with additional comments and responses to the comments.

3. Create and curate content widely

You should also create your own content or sometimes curate content that you find interesting. Share these with your followers and make it easy for them to share with others or post comments.

4. Import your contacts

You probably have plenty of contacts on other platforms. Some of the best sources for useful contacts are your email contacts and phone address book. Start with popular locations like Outlook and Gmail then move to your phonebook. You can then check other online platforms like LinkedIn, Facebook, Instagram, and all the others. This way, you will easily build a decent following in no time. Your followers are likely to have followers of their own. The multiplying factor will mean that you will gain even more followers.

5. Always keep it positive

While on social media, you should always try and present the best side of you at all times. A good social impression is likable and will attract others. There are a couple of things that you need to do to maintain a positive impression of yourself and your brand. Your social media platforms should always be viewed as a reflection of your personality and professionalism.

Make sure that you avoid being argumentative and stay away from any racial and inflammatory religious comments. Also, choose to be very careful when making political comments because others may disagree with your views, or even worse, take offense to your comments. Should it come down to it, then consider having two different social media accounts where one is personal and the other is specifically for your business and brand.

6. Join a couple of groups

Some of the best ways to thrive and grow on social media are through groups. Social media websites such as Facebook and LinkedIn have numerous groups which you can join. To find a relative group, use the search bar on the first page of each social media. Once you join a particular group, you can then engage the members as well as share interesting posts that you come across with your followers. You will not gain any benefits if you join a group and then become dormant. Consider being an active member and participate in discussions and debates. Provide your unique views and opinions to topical issues being discussed then share some of this with your followers and audience.

Product Launch on Social Media

The weeks and days leading up to a product launch can be rather hectic and exciting at the same time. However, the most crucial part of a product launch should be getting the word out. Think about a tree that falls in the forest. Does it make a sound if no one is around? The same question applies to product launches and this is where social media platforms come in handy. Social networks help to get the word out there.

Social media has altered completely the face of advertising. When used correctly, social media can actually help to boost a product. Social sites like Facebook and Instagram are excellent for product launches. There are reasons why such launches are so successful and it is important that these reasons are noted.
Build anticipation

Yet another crucial aspect of a product launch is building anticipation. This means throwing hints around, posting product images, and generally creating hype around the launch. This will create a buzz across different social media and thousands of users will set the ball rolling by discussing the set launch as well as your brand and products. However, you need to be careful with an anticlimax release because these can hurt your brand. Also, ensure that you have the capacity to handle a huge demand once your product launches.

Word of mouth

One of the most effective methods of getting the word out and advertising a product is through word of mouth. Social media sites capitalize on this and help to get the word out there to hundreds of millions of people. As an online business owner, you need to be strategic with your approach.

Start with the right wording followed by strategic placement. If done correctly, a social media campaign can propel your project to a massive audience who will gladly receive it. The most crucial aspect of the entire process is to let others within the social networks to pick up on the buzz and excitement and help to spread the word.

You can actually sit back and watch as the masses pick up the campaign and spread the word to their networks. Others will share within other networks and within no time, the comments will start coming in. It is also advisable to contact influencers and let them test drive your product and see what they have to say.

Attract early adopters

It is advisable to attract early adopters to your products. Tech products are especially attractive to this breed of individuals. They actually love to be among the first to try out a new product in the market and then provide reviews on social media and weblogs. When you attract the early adopters, they will very shortly thereafter become your marketing champions well ahead of time. You should allow influencers a sneak peek at your products and let them leak the information to their thousands of online fans and followers. This will help create an important buzz and hype the market so they are eager to receive and use your products.

Targeting your market

One of the benefits of using social media is that there are settings that allow you to target a certain section of the market. It is a fact that most social media users are between the ages of 18 to 35.

This age bracket is tremendously influential when it comes to the success of a newly launched product.

It is also possible to use social media to target other sections of the market including older generations. While a sizeable percentage may not be on social media, using the influencers and young populations to push a product will eventually have a huge impact on the older generations. This approach is much more successful compared to traditional product launches.

Social Media Marketing and Small Businesses and Franchises

One of the benefits of social media is that it has leveled the playing field such that smaller brands are able to compete equally on the same platforms as their much larger counterparts.

Small businesses are often looking for new and effective ways of getting their businesses and brand out there so that potential customers can find them. If you are not already using social media, then you are losing out in a major way. Social media is great for your business as it provides you with an avenue to attract new customers while engaging current ones on a regular basis.

As a matter of fact, small businesses have a huge advantage over large businesses when it comes to social media marketing. The reason is that to be effective, you really need to engage with followers, customers, and the general public. A business that does not engage with its followers and customers will not enjoy any success on social media.

Small businesses and social media

Interacting with consumers on social media is a crucial marketing strategy for all businesses but especially small businesses. According to a study, over 90% of marketers claimed to use social media for their work. Most of these marketers happen to be working for small businesses. To be successful on social media as a small business owner, you need to set up a schedule to occasionally engage with your followers.

How to Use Social Media for Franchises and Social Media

1. Begin with a modest focus: As a business owner seeking to attract new customers and an impressive following, you will probably get tempted to open up accounts on all known social media sites. However, you should hold back on this approach. Instead, open only one social media account and focus on it for a while. Only after you have learned the ropes can you proceed and open up additional accounts on other platforms.

2. Create a blog: One of the most useful platforms that can help with your social media marketing efforts is a blog. If you already have a website then setting up the blog is easy. However, it really is advisable to have a separate website for your blog.

A blog is a fantastic platform where you can create engaging content which you can then share with others through your social media accounts. Your readers are also able to share the content on their social media sites via sharing buttons provided.

You need to create engaging and interesting content for your blog and social media pages. Content marketing is an exciting new tool popularly used by businesses to market their brands and products. This is why content is so important. Basically, you need to engage your followers on a regular basis with exciting and interesting content. This kind of interaction with your followers will keep them engaged and loyal to your brand.

3. Create a content calendar: It is a great idea to plan your posts so that your engagements on social media are regular and coordinated rather than irregular and abrupt. You should try and plan your social engagements at least one month in advance. In the meantime, you can always search other social networks or websites for suitable content to share with your followers. Try and engage them about 4 times each week or thereabouts.

Be careful not to post too often as this might be considered spammy and annoying. However, keep in mind that certain times of the year are more appealing to consumers, including your followers. These include the New Year, the start of spring, summer, Memorial Day, holiday season, Thanksgiving and so on. You should capitalize on these holidays to increase your brand awareness and even sales.

4. Take the time to build an audience: It takes time and effort to build a reasonable following on social media. Most of your followers will only follow you if you directly invite them. Therefore, take the time to find followers and build an audience. Also, your followers will expect to receive fresh and engaging content every 3 to 4 days from you. It takes about six months for your followers to trust you and start buying your products. In that time, they will share your content with their networks and followers and also bombard you with questions about your products.

5. Measure your success: Once you start getting a sizable following on social media and conversion into leads and sales, you should start measuring the effectiveness and success of your efforts. What you need to do is to track results so that you find out how many of your new customers originate from social media sites. If they are engaging on social media, then you need to get in touch and find out more information about them. Tracking the performance of your social media is essential for your success.

6. Learn more about advertising before paying for it: Sometimes it is necessary to advertise on social media. Paying for advertisements is advisable, however, do not just dive into it. Instead, take the time to learn about social media advertising. Also, ensure first that you have a sizable following before placing adverts. If you simply jump into advertising without careful planning and consideration, then you are very likely to lose money.

Reasons Why Small Businesses are More Successful on Social Media

1. They are focused more on communities and the individual:
There are huge differences between small businesses and large corporations. For instance, large companies have huge numbers of employees, numerous legal and administrative structures with major decisions being made at the headquarters far away. However, there are some differences that are even more fundamental.

For instance, small businesses tend to focus more on individuals and communities. They employ locally, sell locally, and their profits remain in the locality. This way, they are able to easily connect with customers. Small businesses are better able to interact and communicate with their followers and customers online. As a small business owner, you can easily manage the comments and other posts on your social media so ensure that you respond to as many comments and posts as possible.

Social media provides an excellent platform where consumers get to discuss different services and products. And remember to always welcome comments, reviews, queries, concerns, and all other engagements from customers. Fostering connections with individuals is pretty easy for small business owners and rather challenging for large corporations. Customers, both potential and current, will have more respect for those who respond promptly to comments and address their views, comments, and opinions.

2. Social media advertising is very cost effective: Conventional advertising is a costly affair. However, things are very different on social media because the costs are almost non-existent. It is possible to conduct an entire campaign from launch to sales without spending any significant amount of money. Social media has hundreds of millions of users so being able to reach this sizable population for only a fraction of the cost of conventional advertising is absolutely significant. And even when you decide to invest some resources into actual advertising on social media, you will be able to select your target audience and the costs will remain low and affordable.

Social media advertising provides an excellent tool for businesses, especially small businesses, for reaching out to their customers and for increasing their sales. You can provide updates to your customers and followers letting them know all about any new products, sales, or promotions.

With social media, you not only advertise to your current customers but also to potential customers. This helps you to get your brand out there and let all interested persons learn more about what you have to offer. You customers and general followers will then become among your biggest brand ambassadors and promoters.

3. Joint social media marketing efforts: Sometimes small businesses come together on social media to run joint campaigns. They collaborate in this manner in order to put their efforts towards similar social media marketing strategies. It is sometimes an excellent idea as a local business to partner with other businesses within the same local area, to send messages to customers within a particular niche. Keep in mind that these are not competitors but businesses that share the same interests and selling in the same neighborhood.

As an example, you can post that your customers who buy your products will receive a voucher that allows them to receive a discount at another local outlet. Another approach could be to team up with another local business and offer discounts and giveaways. Competitions are also popular where winners receive a prize from participating companies. When you team up with other companies, you will also be building brand awareness and encouraging your customers and followers to also buy from the other businesses. This also attracts more customers to your store.

4. Personalized attention to customers: Small businesses love to pay personalized attention to their customers. For many consumers, shopping at a small business provides them with an excellent experience. In fact, a majority of consumers love to shop at local stores because they receive personalized attention. As the business owner, you should take your time to connect with your customers on an individual basis.

Please note that personalized attention should not be limited to in-store customers only. It should also be applicable to customers who shop at your online store. Ensure that you engage your customers on social media on a personal level and avoid scripted responses that are the preserve of large corporations. Such corporations sell all across the country and have no time to provide personalized responses to clients. This is where small businesses gain the upper hand. You are able to write genuine responses to customers and address their specific situations. This gives you and other small businesses a definite marketing advantage.

5. Small businesses can take advantage of big advertising: There are certain large marketing and advertising events held occasionally. Small businesses can leverage these events into their social marketing strategies. Take for instance the Small Business Saturday or SBS. This is a day set aside to celebrate and promote small businesses across America. It takes place on Saturday following Thanksgiving. Since plenty of consumers are aware of this day, you can leverage by promoting your products and maybe giving discounts so as to encourage customers to buy your products or use your services. This gives you a massive opportunity to gain customers and make sales.

Remember to keep your brand and business names the same across all platforms. Doing so enables social media users to easily find you. This means your current and prospective customers will easily be able to identify you while others will get to learn about your business and your products.

Why Do People Fail at Social Media Marketing?

By now, you know that having a presence on social media is crucial for your marketing and advertising campaigns. You also understand that social media presence is essential for your overall success as a business. Statistics show that seven out of every ten Americans are on social media, so engaging with them on these platforms is absolutely essential.

When it comes to social media, business owners need to understand that there is a lot to learn. There are a number of different social media sites and it is crucial that you identify perhaps two or three that are most crucial for your campaigns. You will need to learn the rules if you are to be successful and have an advantage over the competition. Unfortunately, small business owners make major mistakes with their social media campaigns, it becomes difficult to make any headway. Here are some reasons why people fail with their social media marketing campaigns.

1. Antisocial tendencies: The main aim of social media is to provide a platform where people get to dialogue, chat, share, exchange ideas, interact, and communicate. However, some business owners choose to not interact with their followers at all. This is akin to holding a press conference but not taking any questions thereafter. You need to ensure that you engage your followers and customers on your social media platforms. Do this by answering their questions, responding to their comments, sharing, re-tweeting, and generally being social.

2. Key performance indicators are missing: As a business owner, you should learn how to establish measurable goals. This applies to all aspects of your business and not just social media. A lot of marketers out there are not really sure what crucial performance indicators to watch out for. They believe likes, re-tweets, shares, and follows are reliable indicators.

It is more important to establish measurable goals that will indicate the performance of your marketing and advertising efforts on social media. This way, you will be able to find out what works and what doesn't. Some of these indicators include requests for direction, phone calls, and so on.

3. Understand the dynamics of different social networks: Sometimes marketers will treat all social media platforms in the same way and use the same approach to market and advertise their products. This is known as a misunderstanding of cultures because each social media is different. Identifying the correct advertising channels is critical for the success of your campaigns. It is just as crucial as identifying where your target market is. For instance, you do not need to get onto social sites like Pinterest or Instagram if you are a web hosting firm. However, if you own a bakery, then Instagram and Pinterest would be ideal for your purposes.

4. A lack of engaging content: It is very important that you provide your followers with quality content that is engaging and relevant. The content can be of any nature ranging from video images to photos to text. The most important aspect is that it is relevant, catchy, memorable, and endearing. Doing this will excite your audience, keep them engaged, and endear them to your business, brand, and products. They will probably leave comments, ask questions, or make queries. When they do, then they should not be ignored. Instead, you should engage them, answer their questions, share and like their comments, and so on. This kind of personal attention is crucial for the survival of your business.

5. A lack of essential resources: While social media is largely free to use, you still need sufficient resources to keep your campaigns running. A lot of business owners assume that they do not need any resources because these platforms are free of charge. The truth is that you will need some resources to run successful campaigns. For instance, you will need to have a website and probably a blog. You will also need to create content regularly including videos and photos. With no resources set aside, you will probably fail on your social media marketing efforts. Therefore, before doing anything, you will need to sit down, plan, and strategize for eventual success.

6. Fear of social media: It may come as a surprise but a lot of people out there have an unexplained fear of social media sites. Actually, this is one of the leading causes of social media failures for businesses. Their fear is mostly that they will post something negative which will probably hurt their brand. Yet not posting is actually one of the biggest mistakes that you can ever make. Using social media for marketing and advertising is a very effective way of growing your business, increasing your profitability, and bringing in more customers. It can be even worse if you have a social media page with your brand and company but with no posts. This is a sign that you are anti-social and do not care much for your customers and the general public. If you have no idea how to conduct your social media campaigns, then you should consult an experienced digital marketer who will guide you and teach you the entire process.

Additional reasons why people fail in their social marketing campaigns

Other reasons why people fail when it comes to social media marketing is when they choose not to acknowledge or respond to posts or comments of others. When you ignore your followers, you will slowly send them away and they will go to search for a more responsive brand. Always ensure that you interact with your followers and fans and respond to their comments and posts.

Sometimes, we choose not to comment on similar posts or platforms. This can be a huge mistake because we just never know where customers may be. A simple comment or post on other people's content can bring on board more followers and maybe catch the attention of influencers. Therefore, as a business owner, ensure that you also post comments on the posts of other people as well.

Something advisable to do is to provide advice or assistance to people on other platforms especially popular ones such as www.quora.com and www.reddit.com. When you provide credible and authoritative information on such sites, you will attract the attention of numerous users. Therefore, make sure you provide a sharing button, as well as a link back to your website.

Chapter 2: Which is the Most Important Social Site?

Your small business needs to be on 2 or more social media websites. If you are not, then you are losing out on numerous opportunities. Social networking websites have numerous tools that you can use to reach out to consumers. Think about the fact that over 70% of Americans are on social media or the other. This shows that your campaigns can reach a wide audience.

Social media enables users, mostly business owners promoting their businesses, to target specific audiences. It enables you to do so at very low costs while reaching an extremely large audience. It is this low and affordable cost that makes social media so popular with small businesses. Not only are the marketing costs low, but the reach is much wider than is the case with conventional marketing channels.

However, you need to note that not all social media sites are suitable for all campaigns and for all small businesses. You need to spend some time and learn about the various social media sites out there and how they function. Taking the time to learn how different social media sites function will give you an advantage over your competitors, as well as the advantage of coming up with the right strategies and identifying your audience.

Tops Social Media Websites for Businesses

1. Facebook: This site is best for all businesses if they are to gain visibility and interact with both existing and new customers.

2. Instagram: This popular social media is known for images and videos publishing. It is ideal for businesses that seek to interact via visually engaging content that mostly includes photos and videos.

3. *Twitter:* Twitter is ideal for businesses that seek to engage an elite and tech-savvy audience with bite-sized information as well as videos and photos.

4. *YouTube:* This video sharing site is ideal for both B2C and B2B businesses seeking to send out video messages to their customers.

5. *Pinterest:* This social media website is particularly suitable for consumer-focused brands that target specific demographics such as women.

6. *Snapchat:* The best social site for brands targeting millennials and the youth who enjoy sending messages in a fun way.

Factors Considered When Choosing Social Media for Business Purposes

1. *Cost:* A good social network should cost nothing and needs to be free. If you have to pay to be on social media, then it may not be worth. There are lots of free yet popular social sites that you can use.

2. *Suitability for small businesses:* Always choose social networking sites that have a proven track record of being effective for small businesses. Avoid those with no known history.

3. *Popularity:* Most of the major social networks have millions of followers. Choose those with a large following as they present you with the best chance of success.

4. *Ease of use:* The best social websites are those that are easy for everyone to use.

5. Advanced features: You are able to achieve a lot more and engage your customers and followers better on social networks with advanced features.

6. Geographic targeting: Most small businesses have a local focus so the ability to target a specific niche of the market or particular geographic area adds lots of value.

7. Age: There are some social networks that are more popular with certain age groups. For instance, Snapchat is more popular with millennials while Facebook is suitable for people of all ages.

Here is a brief look at popular social media

Facebook

This is the oldest yet most popular social network in use today. Facebook is superbly popular and is far-reaching with billions of users from all over the world. As a business, you have numerous options to choose from including opening professional pages, placing targeted advertisements, or paid posts for promotional purposes.

Every business should have a Facebook page due to its popularity. When used the right way, it can become an invaluable part of any businesses in terms of marketing, strategy, sales, and customer service. Facebook is an ideal platform for sharing almost all kinds of content ranging from images to stories to videos and memes.

If you open a business account, you will have access to powerful tools that will support your advertisement and promotional campaigns. You also get to enjoy plenty of customization options enabling you to achieve a variety of objectives such as highlighting your contact information, hours of operation, services or products offered, and business address.

Facebook is ideal for people of all ages including seniors. A lot of people aged 55 years and above have Facebook pages which they use on a regular basis. It is also ideal for those seeking small niche markets and foreign markets.

Instagram

This social networking site is also extremely popular and is second only to Facebook. It has been around for quite a few years now and has proven to be reliable and effective in that time period. The largest demographic on this platform includes millennials and teenagers while the least popular are seniors. However, internationally, Instagram has a following very similar to that of Facebook.

Instagram largely relies on photos and images. This is its most distinct feature. Therefore, to be successful on this platform, you need to use high-quality images and photos. You can also upload videos but text content is hardly consumed on Instagram. It is almost entirely mobile which means most users access it via mobile devices such as tablet computers and smartphones.

The platform is more suitable for displaying of artistic work and any products that are best displayed visually via photos. Those providing certain intangible services such as web design may not find this website very useful. It is ideal for marketing to international markets, millennials, and women. The challenge for most small businesses is the ability to produce high-quality content, particularly videos and photos that are appealing to the audience found here.

The audience on Instagram consists of suburban and urban millennials, young people, and teenagers. There are also a lot more females than males on the website making it an ideal platform to target female followers and customers. Since this platform is mostly mobile, the tools and applications are mostly supported on mobile platforms. You will not be able to accomplish much on the desktop version even though there are application programs that can help you with that. Such apps include Buffer and Hoot Suite. You can use these to help you take photos, upload, and edit them on a PC computer.

Depending on your industry, Instagram can be an excellent platform to showcase your products and brand. Therefore, think about your products and if they look good physically, then you should take photos and share with an audience on Instagram. If your work is artistic such as a shoe or clothes designer, a chef, jeweler, and so on, then this is the ideal platform for your business.

As of 2018, the average Instagram user spends about half an hour on the platform each day. And with over 800 million users each day, you stand a great chance of attracting numerous followers, possible leads, and even new customers. You can post a photo and about 3 to 10 stories each day about your brand. There are ways of driving followers, users, and customers to your app so take the time and learn some more about driving customers to your Instagram page.

Twitter

This platform is great for some businesses but not for all. This is why you need to understand different social media. Twitter is awesome for mini posts and sharing links to blog posts and articles. The platform is designed to allow users to post short messages known as tweets. However, you can also post links, images, videos, polls, and much more.

Twitter is ideal for businesses that target a tech-savvy audience, elites, intellects who love brief but precise messages and information in bite-sized chunks. Keep in mind that this is the world's third largest social media platform so doing well here can be a huge blessing. As a business owner, you should set up a Twitter business page and start reaching out to customers and other members on the platform. When you do, you will be able to gain a presence and thereby establish a brand identity.

The ideal posts to share include business information, launches and events, time-sensitive updates, shout-outs, and to re-tweet other people's posts. It is advisable to post between 1 and 3 times each day to more than 275 million monthly visitors.

To create an account on Twitter, simply go to the Twitter for Business page and then simply sign up. Once your account is up and running, you should start following major brands, influential individuals, as well as users within your niche. You should also begin posting updates and provide links to useful content and helpful articles. Re-tweeting is also highly advisable so re-tweet any content that you find interesting, catchy, exciting, and so on. Remember that there are customers out there who rely on platforms such as Twitter to communicate with brands and receive customer service.

If you have a very visible brand or perhaps you do not own a blog, then you may wish to skip this platform. Please note, however, that there are numerous companies that thrive on this platform. This is because of their unique products and brand as well as a distinct voice. Try and set yourself apart so that you stand out among the rest. Companies thrive on Twitter when they engage their customers and listen as they express themselves and share their concerns.

If you can produce exciting and catchy content, then Twitter is an excellent platform for getting the word out to the general public. There are tools that can help you achieve this such as Hash-tags. A hashtag will help to boost your post and attract the attention of numerous others who will read and possibly share your post. With this platform, you should endeavor to find balance. You should share content, posts, and so much more but remember to also share posts from other brands and from your followers.

LinkedIn

While LinkedIn may not necessarily be the most popular social media site out there, it still receives over 260 million visitors each month. It is among the best professional networks available and is excellent for identifying top talent as well as presenting yourself and your brand as professional outfits, reliable, and up to the task. This is why it is known as the ultimate social media site for businesses and professionals. A lot of users refer to LinkedIn as a user's online resume.

It is also a platform where business-to-business interactions occur and where professionals meet and network. The audience on this social media is consists of professionals from all industries. There are approximately 500 million active accounts. As an account holder, consider posting content onto the site about 1 to 4 times per week. Your posts should focus more on product launches, business activity, any interesting but relevant content, and links to content elsewhere off the website.

If you use this website well, you can get in touch with industry leaders, attract buyers, and make sales. You may even proceed to become a thought leader and respected guru in your industry. When you become a respected leader in a particular niche, you are bound to attract more followers and definitely higher sales.

It is advisable for every small business to create a LinkedIn business page. This platform is excellent for businesses and professionals and will expose your brand to all the right people. Getting on LinkedIn also means that you have a credible presence on a professional networking website. As soon as your page is up, you should start sharing content with others as well as posting relevant posts.

You can use LinkedIn in numerous other ways such as headhunting for talent and sourcing potential hires. Most users on the platform design their profiles to resemble resumes while companies create profiles that showcase their businesses. You should ensure that you portray yourself in a manner that brings out information about your company culture. Consider joining industry-related groups when you can interact with firms and professionals within the same sector. This way, you will get a chance to answer questions and present solutions so that you are eventually recognized as an industry leader. It will also bring more followers to your website and company's page.

YouTube

Yet another popular social media site is the video sharing platform YouTube. This site allows users to share, upload, view, comment, and rate video content. The website is now owned by Google and remains very popular with users all around the world. It has become well known as a site for news, information, and entertainment. YouTube's main users are general consumers doing general research and those seeking both information and entertainment. There are over 3 billion searches conducted on this platform each month and almost 1.6 billion active users each month. With such an enthusiastic following, it makes sense to have a page on YouTube and take advantage of the marketing opportunity provided.

One of the most outstanding features on the platform is that members share educational, creative, and visual content. Creativity is really what drives the website and gets users coming back time and again. Upon joining the website and setting up your business page, you should then start producing high quality, creative, and informative videos that will get your message out there and get users to follow you so that within no time your page will have a large and faithful following. It is advisable to post about 1 to 3 videos each week to keep your followers engaged.

As the world's second largest search engine behind Google and the largest video sharing platform in the world, YouTube provides businesses with an opportunity to reach out to consumers. It is especially suited for businesses that can use videos to reach out to their followers and press a point home. If you can teach, educate, or inform via videos, then YouTube is the ideal platform for your business. Think about a landscaping company that teaches followers how to plant a specific flower or shrub.

However, YouTube does require some effort and time compared to other social networking sites. Since this is a video sharing website, you will need to take the time, effort, and skill to custom your videos. You might probably need assistance with the videos at first. If you are unable to develop quality content, then you can seek help from a third party. Alternatively, you may want to get some video editing software to help you with your content.

You should ideally focus on developing between 5 and 10 videos then post at least one each week. Videos vary in length from three to about 10 minutes long. They do not necessarily need to be entertaining but can be instructional or informative. Apparently, a good number of videos on the website are interviews, animated explainers, and how-to videos.

Snapchat

One of the newest but still popular social media sites is known as Snapchat. This is a mobile-only visual network whose content is limited by time. Therefore, it is rather different from other social platforms in this aspect. Members and users of this application program send different posts such as video and photos to each other and sometimes publish content on their public profiles. These last no more than 24 hours.
You can now chat on Snapchat and also send messages, share images and store them, and also share media content and events. While the app is designed to maintain published content for a period of only 24 hours, you are able to save any content that you like onto your mobile or another device. Therefore, you can view content on your Snapchat account and then share the content across other platforms.

One of the benefits of this network compared to others is that there is less pressure on creating superbly polished content. This is due to the content's temporary nature. You also get to know or see which of your followers viewed your content. A prominent feature of Snapchat is the Stories feature. Your small business profile will probably make use of this feature a lot. The challenge is that your videos or other content can only be viewed by users who follow you. Therefore, focus on getting followers so that you have an audience for your content. With the Stories feature, you are able to easily create quality and interactive content.

Google My Business

This specific platform is designed specifically for businesses. Google My Business, therefore, affords you a platform where you can showcase your business, your products, and brand to followers. The main audience on Google My Business is any Google user who is searching for a local business for specific products or services.

On this platform, you will be expected to create a thorough and clearly defined business profile. Such a profile should clearly indicate your business ventures, the services you provide or products that you sell, as well as contact information. Google My Business receives monthly traffic of about 3.5 billion searches each day. However, you do not need to regularly post content or share with others. The main purpose here is for users to find your business.

Google My Business is more like a business directory. It allows your business to display on Google Maps and also appear in local queries. Users are able to rate your business and leave recommendations. Many refer to this social network as the world's biggest business directory. It therefore makes sense for any business, large or small, to list here and establish a presence especially if the business has a physical location.

To get listed, you first need to create a listing. This listing will make it easy for customers to find any information about your business including business name, address, contact information, and the products you sell or the services that you provide. As soon as you claim your location, customers will easily be able to locate you over the internet, make recommendations to other customers, and also identify certain specific features that may attract them to your store.

You need to ensure that you provide as much information as possible on your business profile. For instance, you need to ensure that you include your opening and closing hours, photos of the premises, a menu or a list of products on sale, and so on. Essentially, any business listed on Google My Business will outrank all other businesses that are not listed.

This is basically because of the local pack that is essential for all businesses-based searches on Google. As a small business owner, especially one with an online presence as well, you will benefit immensely by having a business profile on such a powerful platform. Creating a profile is easy, fast, and takes very little time. With Google being the world's largest search engine by far, your marketing efforts will greatly benefit from a listing here as well.

Chapter 3: Marketing and Advertising

To most people, marketing and advertising mean one and the same thing. Even some marketers believe there is only a thin line between the two. However, the two are different even though they share similar objectives. The objective is to inform the public about services and products being sold.

While both marketing and advertising have plenty in common, there are some notable differences. It is crucial for businesses and their owners and managers to comprehend the differences as well as similarities in order to strategize for sales and customer acquisition.

The Distinction between Advertising and Marketing

It is not surprising that there is confusion about marketing and advertising. They are very different even though they aim to reach customers through the promotion of goods and services. If you understand the difference between the two and then conduct your market research appropriately, you will then be able to get your business right on the pathway to success.

Marketing

The term marketing refers to a comprehensive process that includes creation, design, brainstorming, planning, research, and strategizing about aligning a service or product with a specific audience in the best way possible.

This means that marketing is the planning, control, and implementation of a number of activities aimed at bringing together sellers and buyers for the mutually beneficial sale and purchase of products and services.

Step-by-step process

You can think of marketing as a step-by-step process. This process begins with a distinct selling proposition where you use a brief but compelling sentence that defines your business.

It is this well-defined message or proposition that will be the guiding theme that will support your efforts in identifying clients who may be interested in what you are selling.

Research and analysis

Marketing involves research and analysis. This means studying your target market, then coming up with designs and language that will ultimately influence this market. You need to come up with mission statements and slogans that best explain your message. These are essential to your overall marketing strategy. In essence, we can break down the marketing strategy into four different components. These are also referred to as the 4Ps and they are product, place, price, and promotion.

Marketing campaigns put forth a message that lets the public know who can use the product and other relevant information. Marketing materials are used to relay this message which in turn creates the personality and tone of the product and brand. Other aspects include distribution and pricing of the product.

Marketing viewed as a pie

Marketing can also be viewed as a pie that is divided into slices. These slices are represented by market research, advertising, public relations, media planning, community relations, sales strategy, and customer service. Therefore, we note that advertising, while very popular and effective, is just one aspect of marketing.

While all the aspects of marketing work independently, they also need to resonate together towards achieving the set goals of the company's objective. The process of marketing is a tedious one. It takes plenty of time as well as research hours in order to run a successful marketing campaign. In short, we can say that marketing is everything a business does in order to facilitate an exchange or transaction with customers.

However, before running any advertising or promotion, you need to conduct market research in order to determine who your target audience is. After the market research, you could find that social media is a much better place to run an advertisement compared to buying space on print or electronic media.

At other times, it may turn out that penning an op-ed in a local newspaper or magazine could have far better results. Therefore, as soon as market research is complete, you should proceed to develop adequate marketing strategies and proceed to reach out to clients or customers the best way possible.

Advertising

We can define advertising as simply the process of getting the word out there about a product or service so that it gets known by an audience. During this process, a description is used to present the idea, service, or product to the public.

The process of advertising involves campaigns in the print and electronic media and lately on digital media. The campaign will entail creative content and positioning in the chosen media. It is crucial that any advertising message is placed on time

Advertising definition

Any advertisement is a public, paid announcement that contains a persuasive message made by an individual or organization to potential or existing customers.

As already established earlier, advertising happens to be only one single aspect of the entire marketing process. It is, in fact, the specific aspect of marketing that involves letting the entire world get to know about your business, products, services, and brand. Just about all advertising messages will have the name of the sponsor as well as the brand.

The process of advertising involves placing advertising messages in different mediums including television, direct mail, billboards, magazines, newspapers, and even on the internet. It is important to note that the world of print media is fast fading so advertisers are seeking new frontiers to place their ads. These include unusual places such as the top of taxis, on walls, bus stops, and so on.

The main purpose of advertising is to get the word out to the consumer. This process involves several stages including the creation of campaigns that are in line with the desires and needs of prospective customers. An excellent campaign will make use of a variety of media in order to create a buzz and generate excitement about the products or services being advertised.

Different mediums are used depending on the targeted audience. For young people such as teenagers and youth, social media sites are best suited for ad placements. For others such as the retired, TV and radio may be ideal. Other consumer groups may be better reached via billboards, newspapers, and magazine adverts. Even then, you are likely to find that most advertising campaigns make use of more than one particular media in order to reach the widest possible audience.

How to advertise

Advertising is simply the process of getting the word out to consumers and the general public about products and services. The process of advertising involves coming up with campaigns that align a company's products and services with the needs and wants of the public. The hallmark of any advertising campaign is the use of a mixture of media in order to best send a message out as well as creating a buzz and excitement for a product or service.

Similarities between Marketing and Advertising

It is crucial to keep in mind that advertising is just one of the many components of marketing. Marketing involves an entire process of preparing products for the marketplace, while advertising is getting the public to know about these products and services.

Advertising makes use of data collected through various marketing strategies. Marketing is very involving and includes both research and practice. On the other hand, advertising is mostly practice. Marketing focuses on market research and consumer behavior, while advertising focuses on creative works including multimedia productions and design.

Getting Started with Marketing

You do not need to be a rocket scientist to be a successful marketer. However, you do need a sound strategy if you are to be successful in your campaigns. There is no single marketing solution for all businesses. Each small business is different from all others. Therefore, you need to come up with a marketing strategy that is best suited for your business.

The nature of your business really does not matter. This is because all businesses need to have a marketing strategy. Therefore, whether you have a consulting business, a café, an auto garage, a grocery store, or a consignment shop, you will need to find ways to bring in customers to your business. If you are to be successful in your endeavors, then you need to understand the process of deciding on a plan, sticking with the plan, and applying the same resources and time needed.

The Marketing Process

1. Get the know-how: The very first thing that you need to do is acquire the know-how regarding marketing. As a business owner, you really need to know exactly what to do because marketing can be a tricky path to navigate. Having the skills and knowledge on how to conduct a successful marketing campaign is crucial. Therefore, take the time to acquire marketing skills that will enable you to market your business and products effectively.

2. *Set goals and plan a budget:* Now that you have the necessary knowledge that you need to define your end goal, then come up with a suitable budget. You really need to know exactly what you want. For instance, if you sell products, you will want these products to get to a certain niche in the market. When customers buy your products, you will make a profit. Therefore, think about what is important to your business and how far you want to extend your reach. Remember to prioritize your goals by defining your most crucial needs and your long-term endeavors.

Marketing is also a numbers game. You need to set attainable goals and have ways of measuring your success. You also need to ensure that you only engage in efforts that will directly or indirectly bring results. Efforts that do not bring in new business are of no use to you. Therefore, have well-defined goals in terms of profit, revenue, costs, new sales, and number of inquiries. These will help you to keep a tab on your marketing efforts.

3. *Identify your target market:* One of the most important steps you will need to make is to identify who your target market is. Apparently, not anyone who is walking and talking is your target market. To determine the demographic that constitutes your market, you need to do a few things including market research and conducting surveys. The data you receive from these processes will then be analyzed and the information will point you in the right direction. You will be able to determine who your target market is and in what niche they are in. It will then be possible to craft or design a marketing campaign around your market niche and target audience.

4. *Marketing is more than just advertising:* There are numerous aspects to marketing and not just posting adverts or creating websites. If you own a small business, you will have numerous

ways of marketing your business beyond advertising. It will benefit you greatly if you find out which marketing tactics work and which ones are not suitable for your niche. Eliminate the ones that do not work so you do not waste any unnecessary funds, time, and effort on them.

5. *Put your customers first:* You need to take time and really get to know who your customers are. When you get to understand them and know what it is that they really value and want, then you will be well on your way towards a successful marketing campaign. Even after you get new customers, you need to keep in touch with them after the sales and let them understand that you are concerned about their welfare. Try and ensure that you stay ahead of the competition by putting your customers' needs first.

6. *You have to spend in order to earn:* As a marketer and entrepreneur, you need to understand the principle that you have to spend in order to earn. Basically, nothing comes out of nothing. In order to gain customers and make sales, you will need to spend some money. Marketing is a huge task and you will need sufficient funds in order to finance these tasks. However, you will reap profits out of your efforts if you spend money where necessary.

7. *Make use of social media:* A lot of consumers today are on one social media or another. Social media has become so popular that people use it almost on a daily basis for different purposes. Some seek information while others look to share information and news items. Many others wish to find entertainment and anything of interest. Learn how to make use of social media and make sure that it becomes a major aspect of your marketing campaigns.

Tools Essential for Marketing Campaigns

If you have the necessary tools to execute your marketing strategy, then no doubt you will be successful. Successful marketing endeavors will attract new prospects to your firm and bring in new business. Therefore, take some time to learn how to apply your marketing tools effectively for the best results. Here are some of the tools that you need to have.

1. A good plan: One of the things that you really need to have is a plan that will support your brand and efforts for many years to come. Such a plan will keep you on track and help you to achieve your marketing ambitions. The plan does not need to be as elaborate as a scientific manual. However, it should be clearly written with a well-defined path and exact steps that need to be taken in order to achieve your business' overall aim. If this plan and strategy are then communicated to your team, then your will business will soon start reaping the dividends of your extensive and elaborate plans.

2. An excellent product or service: Any marketing or advertising campaigns will not bear much fruit if you do not have an excellent product to offer your customers. Therefore, make sure that you have a high-quality product that actually solves a problem that your customers have and provides a lasting solution. To achieve this, you will need to listen to your customers and take their opinions into consideration.

3. A presentable brand: Having a professional brand is absolutely essential for your success. A brand is much more than just your company's logo. It entails a lot more including what people get to hear and talk about, as well as feel and think about your business. Make sure that you put together a budget that will support your efforts in building a powerful brand. You need to make sure that your brand will stand out from the crowd.

4. An excellent pitch: As a business owner, you can expect numerous individual to ask you over and over again about your business and your products. You need to be ready with quality, interesting answers that will intrigue them. Avoid making the mistake of replying with long, boring answers that will drive your potential customers away. Prepare a pitch and make it interesting, fun, and exciting. Then make sure that you are able to deliver it anytime anyone asks about your business regardless of where you may be.

5. *A professional website:* As a business owner, one of the most important tools that you must have is a brilliant and presentable website. The website should attract users and offer them value. Your business website should be used to acquire, retain, and maintain contact with customers even as you continue reaching out to more consumers. You should learn to embrace the online world early as this will greatly enhance your marketing efforts and give you an edge over your competitors.

6. *Maintain a simple database:* Any successful marketing campaign or strategy should have at its core a solid database consisting of current, past, and possible customers. This makes it easy to keep track, maintain contact, and reach out to them depending on what a situation may call for. It is also possible to maintain interaction through email marketing and communicating via newsletters, phone messages, and so on.

How to Do Your Research

If you have a business and need to reach out to customers, then you need to do some research. Market research, when done correctly, will give you a clear image of the kinds of products and service your customers need and those that are profitable.

If the products or services already exist, then market research will reveal whether these products or services are meeting the needs and desires of consumers. Small business owners should take the time to research different topics and specific questions. This way, they will learn where to make changes, where to improve, and basically what works.

You really should take the time, resources, and effort to perform adequate market research. Failure to do so is like driving a vehicle from Kentucky to Washington with no street signs or a map. You will simply be driving without directions. A good market research campaign will show you who your customers are and where they are located. It will inform you when they are likely to purchase your products or use your services.

The outcome of your market research will enable you to come up with a marketing and business plan. You can also use the results to measure the success of any existing market plans. As a business owner, you need to be extra careful in order to ensure that you ask the right questions. If you do, then you will probably receive the kind of solutions that you need.

Process of conducting market research

- Define your customers
- Engage your possible customers
- Come up with the research questions
- Compile a list of all possible competitors
- Write down a summary of the research findings

Types of Market Research

1. Primary research: Primary research is conducted with the aim of collecting data after an analysis of current sales as well as the effectiveness of current practices. This research also considers the plans of your competitors so that you gain insights about the performance of your competition. The process of collecting primary data involves the following;

- Surveys conducted via email or online
- Interviews conducted face to face or via the phone
- Filling out questionnaires by mail or over the internet
- Gathering consumers into focus groups and getting their opinions

Examples of the kind of questions that can be asked to consumers

- What do you like or dislike about the products or services currently in the market?
- What are the factors that you take into consideration when buying this product or paying for this service?
- Are there any suggestions you have for improvements?
- What should be the price of this product or service in your own opinion?

2. Secondary data: You need secondary research in order to conduct an analysis on data that is already published. Secondary data enables you to establish benchmarks, identify the competition, and also your target segments. Segments, in this case, refers to members of the public who lie within your targeted demographic. It includes those showcasing certain behavior patterns and those leading a particular lifestyle.

Data Collection

One of the most crucial aspects of any small business should be data collection. According to experts, no small business can thrive without understanding its products, its customers, and the services it offers. There is a lot of competition out there so it is highly advisable to regularly collect data from consumers and conduct relevant research in order to keep up. Without research and data collection, you will lose any advantage to the competition.

There are basically two types of data. We have qualitative data and quantitative data. Quantitative data collection methods make use of mathematical analysis. They demand large sample sizes in order to provide reliable and accurate outcomes. Outcomes of data analysis often highlight statistically significant differences. If you have a website, you can receive quantitative results through web analytics.

Web analytics will inform you about the kind of clients visiting your website, the source of your visitors, the amount of time they spend on your website, and even the last page they visit before leaving your website. Qualitative data collection methods enable you to develop and improve your quantitative research approach. They are useful to businesses as they help in defining problems. They often adapt interview methods to find out more about customer values, opinions, and beliefs.

Data Collection Process

You first need to determine who your customers are. This is also referred to as buyer persona. Therefore, take the time to understand who your customers are. They have certain characteristics. These include the following;

- Age and gender
- Job title
- Location
- Income
- Family size
- Major challenges they experience

You will have to engage your target audience at some point. However, you cannot get in touch with all your customers or the entire market. Instead, you will need to identify a representative sample of the target persona. Engage them through individual phone interviews, with online surveys, and in person through focus groups.

There are certain characteristics that your buyers have. You will need to determine which ones to contact and interview. From your buyer persona data, try and identify about 10 of them. Make sure that the ones you select have recently interacted with the business in one way or another. Also, ensure that you have a thorough mix of personas. This means identifying customers that have actually purchased from your business, those that have not purchased anything at all, and those who bought from the competition.

Other points that you need to note

Once you have done your research, you will generally find out what your customers like, love, enjoy and prefer. They will also let you know their preferences about what they like to hear, see, read, and listen.

Your research will reveal a couple of things about your competition and what keeps him or her in business. When you find out this information, make sure that you use it to your advantage. This means learning what works for him and copying, then understanding what doesn't work and ignoring it.

Use social media to gauge customer feelings

Some of the best places to obtain information about your customers and their opinions are your social media pages. This is because your customers often stop by to read your posts, view your content, and leave comments and queries.

If you need information about their feelings on certain products or services, then these platforms are a source of invaluable information. Check their interactions with your page to find out what they like, what they are unhappy about, what could be done better, and things of that nature. Social media is an excellent source of data and information that your business could use.

Steps to help you spend your market research funds wisely

First, you need to make a determination about the kind of information that you need. This is the information that you can use to make serious decisions about your business and its activities. Once you obtain these results, you should ensure that you prioritize them. Focus more on information that will give you the fastest and best outcomes.

Make sure that you review research options that are less costly. There are plenty of these in the USA including Small Business Administration and Small Business Development Centers. There are also trade associations and others so pause and consider some of these factors.

Common Marketing Mistakes Entrepreneurs Make

1. Using web-based resources only: There are some business owners who rely solely on web-based resources to obtain information. While such data is useful, it is generally available to all other businesses, and on its own, may not add much value. Instead, you should use additional resources including small business centers, local libraries, and so on.

2. Using secondary research only: Secondary research is useful but it mostly consists of information obtained elsewhere. Such information from published work of others rarely gives the full picture. Most of it can be outdated and may cause you to miss out on numerous factors that are essential to your business.

3. Surveying only people known to you: Sometimes business owners choose to only interview or conduct surveys with people personally known to them. They could be colleagues, family, friends, and so on. However, such folks rarely constitute the best source of information. It is advisable to receive information only from credible and reliable customers regarding their needs and wants.

Chapter 4: Social Media Marketing

Introduction to Social Media Marketing

The term social media is a general term that refers to totally different websites that provide platforms for social actions. For instance, Facebook is a website and social network that enables users to share photos, updates, videos, stories, links, and so much more. On the other hand, Twitter is yet another social network even though it is drastically different from Facebook. It essentially allows users to share short snippets, links, and updates.

Social media marketing provides a powerful avenue for businesses of all sizes to access and address customers and prospects. Most customers are on social media already and are interacting with lots of other brands. Therefore, if you are not reaching out to them via social media, then you are losing out big time. Using social media for marketing purposes is bound to bring you remarkable success. You will be able to create an amazing and respected brand and even drive sales and leads.

How social media marketing helps with marketing goals

The best part about social media is that it can be your business' best friend. You can use it adequately to achieve a couple of goals. These goals include some of the following:

- Increasing brand awareness
- Building and enhancing conversions
- Increasing web traffic
- Creating positive brand association and identity
- Enhancing interaction and communication with an audience

Basically, the larger and more engaged your social media audience is, the easier things will be for you. This will ensure that you achieve most of all your marketing goals. There are numerous social media websites out there. You can use one or more of these websites for effective marketing campaigns. We will now examine some of the more popular social media sites one at a time.

Instagram Marketing

Instagram marketing can be described as a form of marketing process where businesses pay to post content on the platform. The aim is to get the marketing message to reach to as many targeted individuals as possible. The ability to target particular demography makes Instagram an attractive social network for businesses of all size.

5 Basics of Instagram Marketing to Get You Ahead

1. Focus on custom audiences and preferred demographics: Instagram allows you to send your marketing messages to a select group of individuals. You can choose who receives your messages in order to improve effectiveness. The selected audience could include customers you have interacted with in the past, individuals on your email list, or even an audience that you created based on preferred criteria.

2. Make irresistible offers: Instagram is a very visual platform and users often spend time viewing different posts including images and videos. With the right kind of content and message, you can take advantage of the platform and attract customers to your platform.

3. Make use of lookalike audience: One advantage that Instagram has is that it can help you identify a similar audience to the one that you seek. Therefore, after marketing to your current audience, you can then find a very similar audience to market to. This is a very effective approach that will help increase your reach.

4. Make use of hashtags: One of the most powerful features on Instagram is the hashtag. This platform is really driven by hashtags so while others may not take them seriously, you really should. They have a powerful way of connecting niche audiences and sharing a message.

5. Make use of custom images: While Instagram is huge on photos and images, stock photos are not allowed so make use of custom images of real people.

Getting Started with Instagram

Instagram has a massive 500 million active users each month with some of the largest audience engagement rates on any social media. For instance, engagement rates are 2000 percent higher than Twitter and close to 60% more than Facebook.

Instagram thrives mostly because it is heavy on video and image usage. Therefore, any business selling visually appealing products or can make use of visual media in their campaigns tend to perform best on this platform. Therefore, once you determine that Instagram is the platform for you, you should then begin the process of creating an account and placing ads for your target audience.

Instagram is effective

It has been shown time and time again that Instagram ads are extremely effective. In March of 2017 alone, more than 120 million Instagram users called, got directions, emailed, or visited websites based on Instagram advertisements. This shows just how effective this platform is.

The benefit of using Instagram is that you are able to target specific users and this often means your audience base. Instagram allows you the ability for your promotions and ads to be displayed to selected individuals. The selection is based on certain factors including interests, location, age, and gender. You also get a chance to create a group for your audience for each ad that you place. This way, you can easily post an ad once it is ready.

The first step on Instagram is to create an account. In fact, you have two different options. You can either use your Facebook account because Facebook owns Instagram or you can open a personal Instagram account. You can then begin from here.

Once your account is up and running, you will need to sign up for a business management account. The process is simple and takes only a few moments. Create a business page for your business and brand. Provide as much information as you can including your contact details, business name, phone number, and so on.

Now that your account is up and running and all the relevant information is provided, you should proceed to create your advertisement. The main focus of your ad is that it should be captivating, enticing, catchy, memorable, and so on. Remember that your followers or audience are visual and will check out any great presentation so create a high-quality video or photos for your advertisement.

Instagram with Facebook

Another option that is available to you is to access Instagram via your Facebook account. You can use your Facebook to achieve your marketing strategies on Instagram. To navigate to Instagram via Facebook, you need to first login to your preferred account. From here, you can then choose what it is that you want to achieve. For instance, you can tweak the settings in order to receive more traffic to your website or link. Here are other things that you can achieve via Instagram marketing.

- Reach
- App installation
- Traffic to your website
- Brand awareness
- Video views

- Conversions
- Engagements

Instagram Marketing Goals and Ambitions

Now, if you are seeking brand awareness and reach, then you need to consider traffic, engagement, app installations, lead generation, video views, and messages. Here is a look at each goal in detail.

Brand awareness: One of the aims of Instagram for most businesses is brand awareness. You want to get your brand out there so people can get to know about your business, brand, and products or services. Instagram is an excellent platform for brand recognition and awareness.

Reach: If you are looking to increase your reach or the number of people who view your posts and ads, then first create the ad and then select your Instagram account. Basically, if you are looking to tell a story, then Reach is really the only choice that you can make. The best part about this choice is that you can take advantage of Facebook features that enable more people to view your posts.

Traffic: You can easily use Instagram to drive more traffic to your website. You can also drive users to your website in order to drive traffic. It is the ideal platform for directing traffic. You will, however, need to select whether to send users to your website or to the app store. Once you do, be prepared for the deluge because traffic will come in plenty.

Engagement: You can expect a lot of engagement on your Instagram account. The engagements will include likes, shares, comments, and lots of other engagements. Basically, if you are hoping for engagements with your Instagram account, you will have a couple of options but mostly via your Facebook account.

Lead generation: We all want plenty of leads because if well managed, they can be converted into paying customers. For lead generation, you will receive a couple of things from Instagram including phone number, user's full names, gender, and email address.

Configure Your Target Audience

Instagram marketing gives you plenty of options as well as lots of objectives to choose from. As a business owner, you do not have to be confined to any single one but can have multiple objectives such as conversions, engagement, reach, and so on. You have probably done this kind of configuration with Facebook.

As an example, you may want to target females between the ages of 21 and 45 living in Los Angeles who are interested in workouts and healthy living. This is very possible on this platform. When it comes to location, you can choose whether to generally choose people within a region, state, or country or go down to the city, suburb, or zip code. You can also choose to exclude certain locations so that your targeting is even more precise. You can also target your audience based on their ages ranging from 13 to over 65. Gender options include men, women, and all. Language option is often left blank unless you prefer a certain language setting. Other options that you have include interests, behavior, and demographics.

Secrets towards Skyrocketing Traffic Reach

There are over 1 billion Instagram users all across the world with numerous engagement levels. As a business owner, you want to attract as many relevant users as you possibly can. Fortunately, on Instagram, this is very possible if you use the right tactics. Here are some ideas for your Instagram account on how to attract more traffic.

Get creative with your hashtags

If you are to be successful on Instagram, then you need to forget the one-word, very obvious hashtag. While these are crucial, you need to learn how to mix-up words and come up with interesting hashtags which tell your story. For instance, you can choose to be outrageous, funny, witty, or ironic. What you need to avoid is a boring hashtag.

Actively participate in popular conversations

Try as much as possible to actively participate in as many numerous conversations or posts as possible. When you do, make sure that you use a mix of relevant hashtags and any other trending hashtags.

Cross-promote your dedicated hashtag

You may have created a super exciting hashtag for your business but unfortunately, no one knows about your hashtag or about you. Therefore, the chances of your hashtag getting shared are close to zero. However, you need to ensure that the hashtag is in your profile. Then take the hashtag offline and print it on as many relevant places as possible. These surfaces could include receipts, signs, print ads, and so many other places. Make sure that your hashtag is as visible as possible so that others get to see it.

Get Descriptive with your captions

We all know that a picture is worth a thousand words. However, words are still absolutely crucial and part of your marketing campaigns. Any time you post content on your page, make sure that you add great captions that are captivating and tell a story. This way, you will thrive and be successful in your marketing activity on Instagram.

How to Build Trust

If you are a business owner, then you really need to build trust. When you do, your customers will trust you and they will keep coming back. The first step is to be truthful in the information that you put out there. You need to be honest and forthwith with your followers and customers.

You need to be authentic: Authenticity means revealing the real you and the real business and brand that you represent. When you are authentic, customers will trust you.

You also need to be human and act human: All too often, large corporations and perhaps some businesses lack the human touch. They tend to provide generic responses to posts on their social media pages and may not provide adequate answers or solutions. Being human means appropriate responses to customers and providing adequate solutions to their challenges.

5 Mistakes People Make with Instagram

1. Account settings are private: Having a private account could be a genuine mistake but a really major error. When your photos and videos are all private, numerous interested users may want to follow you or get to know about your business. Ensure that they have access to your page by making it public.

2. Sharing random photos: Sometimes we are tempted to share almost anything with our followers. While this may sound social and friendly, it is actually wrong. A business account should remain professional. Only post relevant photos and videos as well as links and content.

3. Use of low-quality photos: As a business, you should not use any poor quality content whether its images or videos. This will harm your brand and make you look unprofessional. Always use high-quality images and videos.

4. Poor use of hashtags: Sometimes we use hashtags wrongly and sometimes we do not use them at all. This is wrong because hashtags are extremely powerful. Learn how to use hashtags and then use them effectively as you interact with others.

5. Inconsistent in posting: Every successful business owner knows that consistency is key. This applies to your twitter account as well. Therefore, make sure that you post consistently about 3 to 5 times each week.

Facebook Marketing

Facebook is the world's largest social media platform with over 2 billion users. There are more than 180 million users in Canada and the US alone who use Facebook every single day. Here are some basics that will put you ahead of others on this social networking website.

5 Basics to Put You Ahead of the Rest

1. Define who your audience is: When you first get onto Facebook, you will seek to connect with an audience who are mostly those that are interested in your brand and products. You need to learn who they are, what their ages are, where they live, and all such information.

2. Come up with goals that meet your biggest needs: You need to come up with marketing strategies for Facebook that actually address your biggest needs. Think about your biggest needs and what Facebook can help you to achieve. Do not come up with unrealistic goals that may be impossible to achieve.

3. Think about the best content mix: As soon as your goals have been set, you will need to start thinking about your social media posts and what the right content mix would be. The best approach would be to ensure that 80% of your posts educate, inform, and entertain your audience. You will then use the remaining 20% to promote your brand.

4. Have an appropriate ads strategy: You need to put a lot of effort into your social media marketing strategy. Growing brand loyalty and an audience does not happen overnight. These processes take time and effort. Take the time and put in the hard work for best results.

5. Ensure that your posts are always fresh: Your followers, including current and future customers, need fresh yet relevant content from you on a regular basis. Make sure that your posts are not old, boring, repetitive, and so on. You may lose followers just for this. Instead, focus on good quality, interesting, and posts a couple of times per week.

How to Get Started on Facebook

Getting started on Facebook is easy. However, you need to be cautious in order to get it right. The first step is to come up with a Facebook marketing plan. This plan will list your objectives and then mention the different ways you will use Facebook to achieve these objectives. Objectives could be to promote your brand, gain more followers, convert leads, retain current customers, and so on.

Once your strategy is in place, you should proceed to open a Facebook business page. Your business profile on this popular social media is really a huge part of your online identity. Therefore, take time to create a professional page that is presentable and with all the relevant contact information. Remember, it is from here that you will engage your contacts and followers.

As soon as your page is up and running, you should begin posting content and sharing it with others. There are numerous kinds of content that can be posted on this social media. They include videos, links, posts, memes, photos, stories, and so on. Remember to keep the content fresh, entertaining, and interesting.

Secrets for Skyrocketing Your Facebook Traffic Reach

Facebook is definitely the platform where your business should be. This is because of the numerous users as well as the great business opportunities the platform affords you. However, many other businesses are also on Facebook battling for the same opportunities. Facebook organic reach has been declining in the past couple of years so a proper strategy in this case is necessary. Here are some tips on how to skyrocket your traffic reach.

Use content that is optimized to generate shares and attract attention

For successful social media experience and increased reach, you should consider using highly shareable content. Such content is the kind that causes users scrolling down the timeline to pause and read your post. Such posts should be so inspiring that readers feel a strong need to share with their followers. You will be rewarded handsomely for your engaging content by Facebook.

Try and post less content

A lot of time, Facebook users believe that more is better. However, people do not like being overwhelmed with content and posts on the timeline. It is crucial to understand the importance of tidbit information. There are those who believe you must post over 30 times each month and share over 5000 links in order to get ahead. In reality, less is more and it is better. Post fewer items but ensure the ones that you do post are of excellent quality.

Increase engagement by boosting your best posts

If you wish to get more traffic from Facebook, then you really need to reach more of your followers. One of the ways of doing this is by boosting your best posts. For starters, you have to produce top-notch content. This is necessary if you are to see any major results. You should expect your traffic to skyrocket if you can create engaging content that is of high quality.

Combine Facebook ads with email and target repeat visitors

If you wish to drive Facebook traffic to your website, then you can use this indirect method for success. You will need to have the right audience for this. Basically, you will first provide a simple way for Facebook users to join your email list. The button to join the mailing list is very visible and the process takes only a few seconds.

Give audience engagement priority

As a business owner, you should seize every opportunity that you get to engage your audience. The reason is that personal engagement is what keeps them coming back. You need to maintain polite, casual engagement and then share or like their posts. When your followers or other Facebook users leave a comment, this is a way of engaging you in a conversation. Make sure to respond to their comment and keep the engagement going. When your audience feels that they are being heard and their opinions matter, they will engage you even further and will become loyal followers and possibly customers.

How to Build Trust on Facebook

Facebook is an excellent place to build relationships and connect with others. You get to interact and share with current and potential customers. However, having a page only is not sufficient. You need to build a strong brand and trust. People need to feel like you are trustworthy. To build trust on Facebook, this is what you need to do.

1. *Start by covering the basics:* Before you begin posting on Facebook, you need to ensure that all your information is on your page. Make sure that you have your banner image, a good profile image, your website address, office address, contact information, and so on. This is what you need to provide at the very least. Provide your followers, customers, and interested persons as much information about your business as possible.

2. *Provide useful, practical, and beneficial information:* As a business owner, you are probably an expert in your field. This means that you know about a lot of things that your followers and customers don't. Therefore, take the time to provide good quality useful tips, information, and advice that will be helpful to your followers.

3. *Use visual images to express your points:* Try as much as possible to use visual images to express your points across. When you use images, especially catchy, clear images, your audience will engage with you more and this interaction will boost your trustworthiness.

4. *Respond to comments, questions, and posts:* Your followers are likely to leave comments on your page. They may comment about something you posted, ask a question, or generally interact with you. Never ignore them when they do. Instead, take the time to respond to their comments and engage with them.

5. *Share positive stories and posts:* Sometimes your customers and followers will post things on your page. Other times, they will share posts with you. When they do, please share with all your other followers. When you share interesting, exciting, inspirational posts, it gives your followers confidence and boosts trust.

5 Mistakes People Make with Facebook

Facebook has the ability to take your business to the next level. But this is only if you do everything correctly. The problem is that sometimes we make mistakes that cost us. Some silly mistakes people make can ruin their image and hurt their brand. Here are some common mistakes that you should avoid.

1. Not engaging your followers: One of the biggest mistakes that people make on Facebook is to ignore their followers. When you have followers, they are probably also supporters, customers, or possible customers. If you post anything on your Facebook page and receive interactions such as questions or comments, always make sure that you respond appropriately.

2. Incomplete profile information: You stand to lose a lot if you do not complete your profile. An incomplete profile with blank sections and incomplete details will present you as unprofessional and unreliable. You should have a complete profile at all times.

3. Not constantly sharing content: When you do not share content consistently, your followers may forget about you or think that your business is probably down. This does not augur well for you. Posting content consistently and sharing it with your viewers is a crucial part of your marketing strategy and brand enhancement. Always share content regularly and maintain a posting schedule.

4. Lack of Call to Action: Never assume that your Facebook followers know the next step to take. After promoting your brand on the platform for so long, you should leave a clear message about what course your followers should take. A good call to action will require them to probably visit your website or take some other action.

5. Insensitive posts: Sometimes people never think about their posts and so they post very insensitive and cruel things. This can be hurtful to your brand and will disappoint numerous followers. Think about an airline company that used the image of a plane crash to promote its brand. This was a huge fail and followers were not impressed. Try and be sensitive and considerate in all your posts.

Tools to Enhance Your Facebook

Hyper Alerts: There is a fantastic tool that you can use on Facebook to create a monitoring system. One such tool is known as Hyper Alerts. This is a versatile tool that notifies you about all incoming interactions such as published posts, messages, and so on. This way you will never have to worry about missing a message and so on.

Custom tabs: Facebook provides custom tabs to help users to add functionality to their pages. There are plenty of ways to use custom tabs. These can be used for functions such as email sign-ups, registration for webinars, products giveaways, and so much more.

#Hashtags: Trending hashtags are great for businesses because they offer a chance for you to gain more followers. If you latch onto a hashtag and use it, numerous other users will notice you and this opens opportunities for others to follow you and your brand.

Content curation tools: Sometimes you may be unavailable to create new content, yet fresh new content is essential for your marketing strategy. There are certain tools you can use for content curation. A good example is Swayy. This tool analyzes the content that you share with your followers on Facebook and then identifies similar content based on certain keywords.

YouTube

One of the most powerful online marketing tools available is YouTube. It can assist business owners to engage current customers, acquire new ones, promote their brands, and generally market the business. And the best part is that YouTube is free to use unless you wish to place ads.

Statistics show that 4 out of 5 or 80% of all millennials use YouTube when researching a purchase decision. This is one of the reasons why video marketing is becoming more and more popular. Here are some tips to help you get ahead.

Create videos based on a single keyword or topic

It makes sense to focus on a niche and then produce video content based on that niche. While this sounds obvious, not many people do this. A lot of people tend to get off-topic and discuss everything under the sun. It is advisable to come up with relevant keywords and then focus on these keywords and niche.

Optimize the description and title of your content

Since YouTube is the largest search engine after Google, you need to optimize your videos so that they rank highly. To achieve this, you need to ensure that you optimize your descriptions and video descriptions. For instance, you need to ensure that you use titles.

Use thumbnails and catchy titles

It has been shown time and again that video content with catchy thumbnails and titles tend to rank much higher even when the content is not that great. Therefore, focus on working on developing catchy thumbnails and titles for your videos in order to get ahead.

Use playlist URLs to increase the time users spend on your channel

At the end of YouTube videos, there is always a list displayed of recommended videos to watch. Some of these may belong to others, while some may be yours. Make sure that you use well-crafted playlists in order to maintain users on your channel.

YouTube will likely queue your videos so that your users may watch them immediately after.

Engage with your viewers and encourage discussions

If your channel has numerous engagements, then YouTube will reward you. Engagements include viewers spending more time on your channel and watching more content. Also, ensure that you engage with your viewers by responding to their comments and answering their questions.

Getting Started with YouTube

It is easy to get started on YouTube and the process is relatively stress-free and simple. Most of the tools that you need are actually free. The first step you need to take is to open a Google account. Most people already have one. If you do not, then you should open one. In the process, you should create a Gmail account. This account will act as your YouTube account.

When you log into your account, proceed to YouTube. You will see the structures necessary to create a business channel. This will essentially act as your video hub. You will then be able to upload videos, select keywords, edit descriptions and titles, and then take a look at the analytics as they inform you about the performance of your videos.

And that is all that you need to do. Now you can begin creating videos for your channel. Try and find a high definition camera or even a good quality smartphone. You will also probably require a tripod for good quality videos, as well as video editing software. Ensure that you invest in a good quality microphone, as well as top-of-the-range sound quality.

Secrets to Skyrocket Your Traffic Reach

It is impressive to note that over 500 million hours of YouTube videos are watched each day. The sad part is that less than 15% of business owners leverage on this viewership to promote their businesses. Fortunately, there are ways available to you to increase traffic to your YouTube channel.

Develop top-notch, high-quality content

There is nothing that can increase your reach and attract viewers to your YouTube channel than killer content. If you want to engage an audience for hours and retain them for a long time, ensure that you routinely develop and deliver high value, informative, and entertaining content.

Optimize your YouTube content

Even YouTube content needs to be optimized. Remember that YouTube is the world's second largest search engine. If you are able to competently optimize your content, then you can expect to attract more YouTube traffic to your website.

Use available tools to increase your YouTube traffic

YouTube provides plenty of tools which you can use in order to optimize your content. For instance, you can use video editing software to help produce quality content. There is also a tool known as Tube Buddy which is designed to help with the management of smaller tasks. These tools will definitely boost your traffic.

How to Build Trust on YouTube

Basically, without regular interactions between brands and customers, some organizations would encounter immense marketing challenges. Platforms such as YouTube provide excellent opportunities for brands to engage with their customers and prospects. Such relationships help to build trust and a community will form around your brand.

Publish honest content

As a business owner, you need to ensure that everything that you do is forthright and honest. Your followers, as well as the general public, will trust you when you are honest and forthright. This also means that you should publish honest content at all times. This is content that comes from the heart. It does appeal to followers so make use of it.

Engage followers directly

Another crucial advice that you need to always apply is to engage your customers and followers directly. Social media is always a two-way street so you need to ensure that you give as much as you take. You should, for instance, respond to comments, ask follow up questions, and also like and leave comments on your followers' posts.

Become an authority

YouTube users are likely to follow you and trust you if they believe you are an authority in your niche. You become an authority when you provide excellent content about a niche continuously for a period of time. If you can answer viewers' questions and address different topics, you will sooner or later be considered an authority in the field.

Provide helpful content

You also need to provide content that is helpful to your community of followers and viewers. A lot of people get onto social media seeking help, guidance, and advice. It is content producers like you that they look up to for assistance. If you can provide helpful content time and time again, then you will be able to gain the trust of your followers.

5 Mistakes People Make with YouTube

Not uploading sufficient videos

When you upload a sufficient number of videos to your YouTube channel, it will remain active and your followers and viewers will enjoy a good experience watching your videos.

The number of videos that you upload to your website will vary depending on the niche, channel, and style. However, you should endeavor to post at least one video each week. Others can manage two or more. Regular uploading is advisable and failure could hurt your brand.

Poor quality audio

Your videos need to be of great quality at all times. This is what will keep your channel active and encourage more and more visitors to your channel. However, a poor quality video will ruin the experience for your followers and viewers may not be happy. Always endeavor to ensure that not only is the video of excellent quality but also the audio.

Not requesting for comments at the end

You should be courageous enough to ask your viewers to leave comments after watching a video on your channel. The best approach is to ask once and politely. You should not beg either. This will make you sound desperate and far from the expert or authority. However, you should feel free to invite viewers to leave a comment then engage anyone who posts a comment.

Failure to break your channel into categories

As you upload more and more video content onto your website, you will notice that you are entering into specific areas but all within the same niche. At this stage, you should start categorizing your videos. If you fail to do so, you will introduce confusion as you will probably have a large list of videos. Viewers will be forced to scroll down for ages to find a useful video. This is not advisable so you should come up with appropriate categories for your videos.

Failure to share your videos on other platforms

Sharing a video on YouTube is advisable but not necessarily sufficient. You will need to also share the same video on other platforms. Other social media sites like Facebook or Instagram should be used to share this content. This will enable you to receive more views as well.

Do not copy or steal other people's titles, hashtags, or descriptions

There are a lot of YouTube users who steal or copy metadata from other users. This is in the hope that they will benefit from the information just as much as the predecessor. Most people get annoyed at this kind of behavior. It hurts your brand and paints you as dishonest. Always come up with your own titles and descriptions rather than copy from others.

Branching out too far on a single channel

Another mistake that people make on their YouTube channels is creating a very broad channel. This creates confusion and your followers may not know exactly what niche you are in. This will result in much fewer subscribers than you actually deserve and will not augur well for your brand and your marketing strategy.

Tools That You Can Use on YouTube

Visuals are very powerful in communicating messages. It leaves a lasting impression and connects very well with audiences. Video content is therefore the most effective and with superior effects. Here are a couple of tools you can use for effective.

1. *Buzz Sumo:* One of the major challenges that YouTube users are faced with is coming up with a topic for their content. A good topic is one that is relevant and one that is trending. Buzz Sumo provides that exact solution. It enables users to come up with the right kind of topics and titles for their content.

2. *Go Animate:* Another great tool that you can use for your YouTube videos is a tool known as Go Animate. This tool helps you to create animated videos in a simple yet exciting way. You are able to come with professionally created videos using basic drag and drop actions.

3. *Canva:* One of the best tools for helping you to create high-quality and presentable images is known as Canva. This tool is excellent because of its ease of use and the high-quality nature of the end product. You can use it to create professional looking banners in different fonts and layouts.

Twitter Marketing

Twitter is definitely an excellent platform to grow and nurture your business. However, things move extremely fast on this social media. Basically, the lifespan of a single tweet is thought to be not more than 18 minutes. This is about four times shorter than a Facebook post. Just think that there are more than 7000 new tweets posted every second on Twitter. Fortunately, there are things that you can do to help you get ahead on Twitter.

5 Basics to Put Your Business Ahead of the Rest

1. Select the right profile photo, handle, and header image

Ideally, you need to ensure that your Twitter handle is easy to remember, recognizable, and pretty short such that people can tag your business onto other posts. Also, ensure that when users search for you on Twitter, they will be able to find your business and its handle. This will lead them to your page. Also, ensure that you keep all your names the same across all social media.

2. Set goals and define success

When you decide to join Twitter, you should have your goals clearly defined. The reasons you get onto Twitter are to:

- Increase customer loyalty
- Generate sales and leads
- Build product awareness and brand loyalty
- Decrease customer support costs

You can use these well-defined objectives to craft goals that can be measured and improved on with time. This way, you will be able to evaluate your social media performance and prove your success.

3. Optimize your bio information and showcase your brand

Twitter basically allows you to showcase your company's bio using only 160 characters right beneath your business' profile photo. Make sure, therefore, that you create an absolutely impressive bio. It is not a difficult feat to achieve. All that you need to do is to explain using a couple of sentences who you are.

4. Research your competition

Even as you put your business on social media, there are probably tens of other businesses doing the same thing. It is advisable to gather as much information as possible. With this information, you will be able to determine which strategies to alter and which decisions to make. Generally, you can choose to copy some aspects of the competition but do a much better job.

5. Tweet during peak hours

One of the best ways of getting ahead on Twitter is to engage during peak hours. On Twitter, there are certain times of the day and days of the week when there are more active users compared to other times. You first need to identify these times and days then focus on placing most of your tweets then.

Getting Started on Twitter

The first step you need to make on Twitter is to create an account. One of the things you need to consider when creating an account is to think about your username. On Twitter, this is known as your handle and it is always outward looking. It is through your handle that the public will identify your business. Check if your business name is available. If it is, well and good but if it is not, try and find a name that's as close as possible.

During the opening account stage, you will need to provide your email, your business name, as well as a password. You should check if any of your friends are on the platform already. Use your email addresses to search for them. Invite as many to follow you as possible.

Tweak your settings from your home page. You need to make sure that you are on the home page before making any changes. Set the time zone to your preferred one and make all other changes or adjustments to the default settings.

Now create a bio that captures the ideals of your business. Twitter is generally one of the most open social networks. This is because all posts and updates happen on the open platform or timeline rather than on individual pages. This means it is much easier for people who have never heard of you to be able to find your business with ease.

You should then upload a photo relevant to your business or any other image you wish onto your profile. Make sure that you do not start posting tweets until you eventually have a profile image. Now, you can send your initial tweet which really introduces you to the millions of Twitter users. Finally, track down and find interesting and exciting individuals and organizations to follow.

Secrets of Skyrocketing Your Twitter Traffic Reach

You need to come up with a Twitter strategy for your brand. As it is, there are numerous ways of benefitting from this micro-blogging platform. Here is a look at a couple of ways to enhance your traffic reach.

1. Come up with a brand new Twitter design

It is said that we only get one chance to present a first impression. On Twitter, this first impression starts with your Homepage design. You need to ensure that people are impressed with what they see if they are to follow you. If they do not like your page and what they see, then they will most likely not follow you. Therefore, come up with and implement a brand new Twitter design.

2. Get Visual

While Twitter is a micro-blogging social media, it is not solely a text-only platform. Users get to post and share numerous images and videos. In fact, Twitter has enhanced images on its platform using a new feature known as Visual Content. This feature automatically expands images accompanying your tweets. Enhanced stunning images go a long way in enhancing your posts and updates which in return enhances your reach on Twitter.

3. Entice your followers

Sometimes the need to share links arises. In fact, link sharing is quite popular on the platform. When sharing a link, try not to give out all information about its content. You do not want to give everything away because most likely your readers will not click at the link. Just a small teaser is sufficient and they will pounce on the link and follow it to your website, blog, or wherever you direct them to.

4. *Follow hundreds of people*

As a small business, your budget is probably limited. As such, generating followers can be a real challenge. However, if you really want to generate more followers, then you should follow hundreds of users. When you follow people on Twitter, they are very likely to follow you back. However, it is important to aim at follows from a relevant type of audience.

5. *Join the conversation*

One of the advantages of using Twitter is that it is a public platform. This is unlike other platforms such as Facebook where conversations are confined between friends. Therefore, you can easily take advantage of Twitter's public platform to join in any interesting conversations. You can search twitter for conversations related to your business and then join these conversations.

Building Trust on Twitter

Like most other social media platforms, trust is key if you intend to promote your business. It is crucial that your followers and all others believe in you and trust that you are actually who you say you are.

In business, trust is everything. You need to make sure that you develop trust with your customers, followers, and all other Twitter users. Here are some ways of building trust within your community.

1. Use a branded background image: One of the first things that people notice when they get to your Twitter profile is probably your background image. You need to ensure that this background image is presentable, looks great, and is relevant to your business. Make sure that this image contains the same branding features found on your website and logo, as well as other social media sites.

2. Add an appropriate profile photo: Apart from the background image, you need to have an appropriate profile photo. This will give your followers and customers a sense of trust if they see an image of the owner or manager of a business. It is crucial that the photo used is both appropriate and appealing.

3. Get verified: If you want to increase conversions as well as enhance trust, then you should ensure that your account is verified by Twitter. When you get verified, you will receive a trust seal from Twitter. Anyone who sees the trust seal will know that you are verified which makes it a lot easier to trust your brand. The simple verified icon from Twitter enhances trustworthiness immensely.

4. Highlight your credentials: Another crucial step that you need to take is to highlight some of your positive attributes. Basically, Twitter allows you to provide personal biographical information on your profile. It is here where you get the opportunity to highlight your credentials and enhance your positive attributes.

5. Connect your business website to your profile: If you have a business website, then you should connect this to your profile. Twitter actually enables you to include a link from your website to your profile. This provides an excellent way of directing traffic to your site. It also enhances the trust that followers have of your business.

5 Mistakes People Make on Twitter

There are certain mistakes that you need to avoid making on Twitter because they can harm your brand or lose you some followers. Here is a look at some of these blunders so make sure that you avoid them at all times.

1. Using too many hashtags: Some users tend to use too many hashtags in a tweet. Not only is this a display of poor marketing skills, but it is also ineffective and distracting. Your tweets will appear spammy and followers will generally avoid them. Try and remain as professional as possible in your tweets.

2. Posting generic questions: Some people have a tendency of posting questions such as, "Hi, how is your day?" First of all, your followers will avoid this question and move to the next tweet. While casual conversations are allowed and actually augur well with followers, it is crucial that you post sensible questions or posts that your followers can relate with and respond with no issues.

3. Irregular activity on Twitter: If you have a social media account on platforms such as Twitter, then you should log in on a regular basis, share posts, participate, and generally be active. However, some people tend to be absent most of the year and then re-appear suddenly and out of nowhere. This is not a good practice at all. You should log into your Twitter account regularly and ensure that you engage your followers, like posts, re-tweet, and generally be active.

4. Retweeting your own tweets: Some of the shady things that people do on Twitter include retweeting their own tweets. This is akin to liking your own Facebook posts. It is shady and you should avoid it. If you have an important point to make, you should find a new way to say it.

5. Robot posts: Most business owners are busy individuals sometimes with very little time to get onto social media and interact with their customers and followers. Sometimes they use a tweet scheduler to post on their behalf. Using this feature in moderation is okay. However, overusing the scheduler too often may harm your brand and actually lose you some followers.

Tools That You Can Use to Enhance your Twitter Experience

Twitter is a great social media for business. Businesses use Twitter for various marketing purposes including advertising, sales, and promoting products and brand. There are a couple of great tools out there that you can use to enhance your Twitter experience.

Hoot Suite: One of the most popular tools on Twitter is Hoot Suite. This is an excellent tool that helps you to stay organized on Twitter. You can use it to launch posts on Twitter and all your other social media platforms.

TweetDeck: This is another great tool for Twitter just like Hoot Suite. This dashboard management tool provides you with the ability to organize your social media platforms including Twitter. This specific tool is owned by Twitter and is not a third party app.

Buffer: This is a fantastic tool that can automatically post content on your behalf as per schedule. It can help with your posts no matter how many they are, how often you need to post, and across the different social networks.

Twitter Counter: As a business, you need data in order to conduct an analysis of your performance. Twitter Counter is an excellent tool that performs basic analytics as well as graphs. These are based on things such as tweets and followers on your page. You can find out how your page is performing per hour, each day, monthly, and so on.

Pinterest

5 Basics to Put Your Business Ahead of the Rest

Pinterest is yet another of the popular social media widely used across the US and around the world. Over 58% of millennials in the US alone are on Pinterest. This social media site receives about 500 million hits each month. This kind of reach should interest marketers. Yet Pinterest is not favorable of marketers. This is possibly because it is relatively new in the market and most marketers are unaware of it.

However, there are numerous bloggers and business owners who are doing really well on Pinterest. There are even bloggers and marketers who rely solely on Pinterest marketing and earn a living out of it. Pinterest is really easy to use. You simply need to understand how it works and you are ready to get started. Here are some basics to get you started.

1. Create a killer profile: As with most other social media platforms, you get started by creating an impressive and outstanding business profile. All too often, account holders on Pinterest tend to go about this the wrong way. Many of them have accounts with just a name but no image or Avatar on their profiles.

2. Provide quality Pinterest ready images: Pinterest is all about images. The better the quality of photos that you use, the more outstanding your profile will be. Keep in mind that Pinterest is a visual site so images are really big.

3. Open an account without an invite: For a long time, people could not open an account on Pinterest without an invitation. You essentially had to wait for an invitation to come through. This caused interested applicants to wait for ages. Fortunately, this has changed and anyone can now open a Pinterest account without having to wait for an invite.

4. Connect to other social networks: Pinterest allows you to share posts and content with users on other social media websites. You can share your Pinterest content on social media sites such as Twitter and Facebook. Your followers and customers can also do the same. Sharing your pins on other social sites will extend your reach and bring in more followers.

5. *Open a business account:* You can open either a business or personal account. A business account has different terms of service compared to a personal account. Also, the business account has access to analytics. Data collection and processing can provide you with useful information about the performance of your account.

How to Get Started on Pinterest

The first step on Pinterest is basically signing up. Upon signing up, you will get an option to link either your Twitter or Facebook page. Connecting is important because not only do you get to share posts across multiple platforms but also invite friends and followers.

Once you sign up, the next step is to create your profile. As you create this profile, think about your other social networks. This is because it is advisable to use a consistent name. This way, it becomes easier for others to find you. It is also advisable to use the same social media profile photo to make others find you easier.

As soon as your profile is up and running, you should go to the settings page and check that everything is alright. You may want to keep your email settings on as Pinterest options are straightforward. When your email notifications are on, you will be able to see who is viewing your posts and who is leaving comments.

You also need to learn how to post pins. This is what you do on Pinterest. This social platform needs users to post pins which are generally images for others to view. The process is simple. You first need to install the Pin It button on to your web browser. There are instructions available on Pinterest on how to launch this button.

As soon as this button is installed, you should begin posting pins. Adding a pin is fairly easy. The Pin It button makes it easy to post pins. You can use this button directly from your browser or the bookmark bar on your browser. Pins are posted on boards so create a board where you will post pins.

Secrets to Skyrocket Your Traffic Reach

As with any other social media, you want to increase your reach, attract more followers, and get more customers. These actions will help to improve the visibility of your brand, increase sales, and promote your business. There are certain things that you can do to extend your reach on Pinterest. Here is a look at some of these.

Link your Facebook or Twitter accounts with Pinterest account

Pinterest allows users to link to other social media. This is a great opportunity to share posts from one platform to another. You can also invite followers from either social media to follow you and to like or share posts.

Like, share, and re-post pins

Another trick is to like and share content from other users. Basically, you need to engage other users especially your followers and customers. When you do this, you will increase your reach and even convert leads into customers.

How to Build Trust

Trust is everything when it comes to business and also personal relationships. Without it, you cannot expect to achieve much. If you want to build trust on your Pinterest account, then there are a couple of things that you need to do.

1. Have a genuine and credible profile: As a business owner, you need to be honest from the word go. This means being truthful and straightforward even on your profile. Therefore, provide your information including contact info so that customers can identify you in order to build trust.

2. Try and use the same name across networks: If you have more than one social network account, try and be consistent across them. This way, your customers and followers will be able to identify you.

3. Tell your company's story: Everybody has a story and so do you. Tell everybody about yourself, your company, and what you do. Make it brief but make it honest and relatable.

4. Use relatable images: Post images that your customers and followers can relate with. These could be images from the workplace with you and your workers going about your work. It could also be all of you at an end-year party or something similar.

Mistakes People Make on Pinterest

1. Using your business account as a personal account: As a business owner, you have to focus on your brand and your business. All too often, we get carried away and start treating the Pinterest account like it was a personal account. This looks and sounds unprofessional and should not happen.

2. Not sharing your content on group boards: If you are on Pinterest, then you should share content just like on other social media platforms. To create awareness and for your business to get known, you will need to share content where others can see it. If you do not, then users may not become aware of your existence.

3. Posting own content more than other people's: It is good to post content on your Pinterest account. You should also promote it. However, you should also share other people's content. This is crucial for your success.

4. Overreliance on automation tools: Sometimes we get so busy that we lack time to spend on our favorite social sites. This is common and happens to almost all business owners. As such, we tend to rely on automation tools. However, you should use these tools in moderation. These tools that assist in posting pins when we are busy should be used sparingly. Overreliance on these tools can harm your brand.

5. Creating new pins for each post: Every time you try out a different template, then you will probably be starting from scratch. This is an inefficient use of your time. It is much easier to create a design that works then use it to create other pins.

Best Tools for Your Pinterest Account

As a business owner, you probably manage more than one social media account. If this is the case, then you need help and the best help comes from tools designed for this very purpose. Here are a couple of tools to help you with your Pinterest account.

Buffer: Buffer is a browser extension that can help with your pins. You can use it to find excellent images to pin from any website. You can then use Buffer to schedule the image so its pinned at an appropriate time.

Tailwind: This is a fantastic management tool that comes with superbly useful analytics options. You can use this tool to find trending pins, analyze your competition, your influential followers, the top re-pinners, and so much more.

Viral Woot: This is a tool formerly known as PinWoot. It gives users a number of options including tools to grow followers, scheduling, and some advertising. However, it is only free at the start, then you will have to pay to use it.

Loop88: This is an interesting tool that simply connects top Pinterest influencers with brands and advertisers. Influencers are basically individuals with an engaged audience and large following. Using this tool will increase your followers and exposure when one of these influencers shares one of your pins with their followers.

Chapter 5: Social Media Advertising

Advertising on social media enables you to reach out to a huge audience with the hope of getting more engagements, increased leads, and possibly even sales. The best aspect of social media advertising is that you are able to target a particular audience and deliver your message to a very specific and possible recipient audience.

Another interesting aspect of social media advertising is that it allows users to test your advertising organically in order to find out what works and what doesn't. And since social media advertising tends to be cheaper, it is a lot more effective with much better results compared to other forms of advertising.

Instagram Advertising

Overview: Instagram ads started in late 2015. Using Instagram advertising, it is possible for marketers and business owners to reach any segment of Instagram's users. There are over 400 million users on Instagram each day. You can use the ads to promote your brand and to increase both engagements and sales.

Instagram makes advertising very easy on its platform. Advertisers can choose the kind of ads to post, the audience to reach, and the length of time that the ad will run. You can also schedule when to have the ads displayed.

Cost and reach: Instagram allows you to target a specific audience. Most users are between the ages of 18 and 34. You will find more women than men on the platform. When it comes to costs, you can choose between a daily or lifetime budget. The daily budget stands for the amount you will spend on ads each day. This amount is usually about $5.00 but no more than $15.00 per day. Lifetime ads for a period of 28 days, for instance, will cost you no more than $140.

Advanced tactics: You have a couple of choices to make regarding ad formats. These include single image, carousel, slideshow, canvas, and single video. You can add a website URL to drive traffic to your website.

Facebook Advertising

Overview: Facebook has over 2 billion users making it an excellent platform for advertisers. Business owners can push their brands and reach out to customers. Facebook is excellent at lead generation and for obtaining email addresses among other things.

Common advertising content used on Facebook include free shipping, product coupons, e-books, whitepapers, and so on. *Cost and reach estimates:* Pricing varies widely on Facebook and the more you spend, the more efficient the algorithm becomes which improves your ad performance over time. The average cost of a CPC ad is about $0.28 per click while cost per impression is $7. You get to choose your audience so you can reach as many people as you want.

Advanced tactics: You need to ensure that you do not run the same ads to all of your audiences. Try and make use of prospecting ads in order to build brand awareness. Test ads often and also make use of lookalike audiences feature.

Twitter Advertising

Twitter is the platform renowned for breaking news as well as providing a platform where users can connect with both mainstream and niche influencers. There are over 328 million users on Twitter each month and it is still one of the most popular social media websites.

Twitter is a platform that enables organic engagements, unlike other major social media platforms. As such, brands do not necessarily have to pay in order to reach out to their customers and followers.

Pricing: Twitter is affordable to most brands. Basically, you can expect to pay around $10 for CPM or a thousand ad impressions and about $0.30 per click. You can expect to receive similar levels of engagement on either of these campaigns.

Advanced tactics: Make use of relevant yet compelling images with your tweets. Ensure that the images draw attention and fit your brand. Ensure that you are absolutely targeted when it comes to lead magnets or products that you decide to promote. Finally, make sure that you build user engagement within the advertisement.

Pinterest Advertising

Pinterest is different from other social media platforms. It uses mostly images and photos, and therefore, is similar in some ways to Instagram. However, it is also quite different from Instagram. It is largely targeted towards women because more than 81% of users are female. Pinterest boasts an impressive 175 million monthly users and is quite active.

Cost and reach: Ads are now cheaper on Pinterest but a short while back they were quite costly. Back then, you'd pay between $30 and $40. However, these prices have dropped drastically. Today, you can expect to pay about $1.50 for CPC ads and about $5.30 for CPM ads.

Advanced tactics: You need to engage with your followers. Like their posts, answer their questions, and comment on their pins. Remember to focus on trends and join in if you come across a trend. Creativity sells so make sure that you stand out by being creative.

YouTube Advertising

YouTube advertising is quite different from other forms of advertising. There are certain constraints on YouTube but a number of options as well. Marketers are now able to target ads at viewers who a while back checked out or searched for a service or product.

Costs and reach: There are generally three types of YouTube video ads. These are TrueView ads, Video Discovery ads, and In-stream ads. The average cost-per-view of a video on YouTube is $0.20. The UDOT costs $1,000 to reach 10,000 viewers. However, a typical video ad costs between $0.1 and $0.3 per view depending on a number of factors such as your target audience, video quality, and overall goal.

Advanced techniques: There are a couple of tools you can use on YouTube in order to benefit your brand even more. First, create your own YouTube channel and place your videos here. Make sure that you optimize your videos so that they can be found by viewers. Finally, you should learn how to use YouTube analytics. This will help you learn about the performance of your ads.

Chapter 6: Hiring a VA for your Social Media Accounts

As a business owner, you will at one point require assistance with the management of your social media accounts. This is especially so if you have another job or occupation away from your business or if your business is growing fast. Under such circumstances, you should consider getting a virtual assistant or VA to help you accomplish some of the chores.

As a small business owner, the time spent on social media can be spent more productively performing other tasks. A virtual assistant will allow you some flexibility and freedom that you really need. There are certain tasks that they can help you with. These include:

- Researching and writing content
- Engaging and monitoring your audience
- Help to build and manage your network
- Manage your Facebook and other ads
- Keep your social media profiles active
- Maintain a social media planner
- Come with a monthly report about your performance across social media
- Run and manage any social media competitions and so much more

There are plenty of tools that your virtual assistant can use to achieve your objectives. Such tools are in some cases free but cost minimal amounts in others. It is much better to use a virtual assistant compared to an in-house assistant. Virtual assistants cost less, charge by the hour, work remotely, and hence maintain professionalism.

Where to Find Virtual Assistants

There are some obvious places where you can find virtual assistants. These include well known remote jobs platforms such as Upwork and Fivver. Upwork is a respected freelancing platform where you can easily find virtual assistants. You first need to post a request, after which, you will receive applications. Vet these applications and find one who suits your needs and has the necessary experience.

There are other platforms apart from Upwork and Fivver where you can find reliable and professional VAs. These include the following:

- Guru at the URL address www.guru.com
- VA Networking located at www.vanetworking.com
- Resource Nation located at www.resourcenation.com
- Popular social media like Twitter and Facebook

Conclusion

As a business owner, you need to take advantage of as many social media platforms as possible. Social media provides your business and brand an excellent chance to grow, reach out to customers, develop your brand, attract customers, provide customer service, generate sales, and so much more.

Try not to jump into all social media platforms at once. Instead, approach each with some caution so that you learn and understand how it works. This way, you will get to know which social networking sites are most suitable for your business and which ones are not.

Once you have your social media pages up and running, you should keep them active. You do this by posting content regularly. You need to make sure that the content you post is relevant and of high quality. Make sure that you remain engaged often. This means you should share posts, follow others, join groups, comment on posts, and always respond to comments on your posts. You should always respond to comments and messages sent to your social network account so as to retain your customers and followers.

www.ingramcontent.com/pod-product-compliance
Lightning Source LLC
Chambersburg PA
CBHW070849070326
40690CB00009B/1759